MW01282956

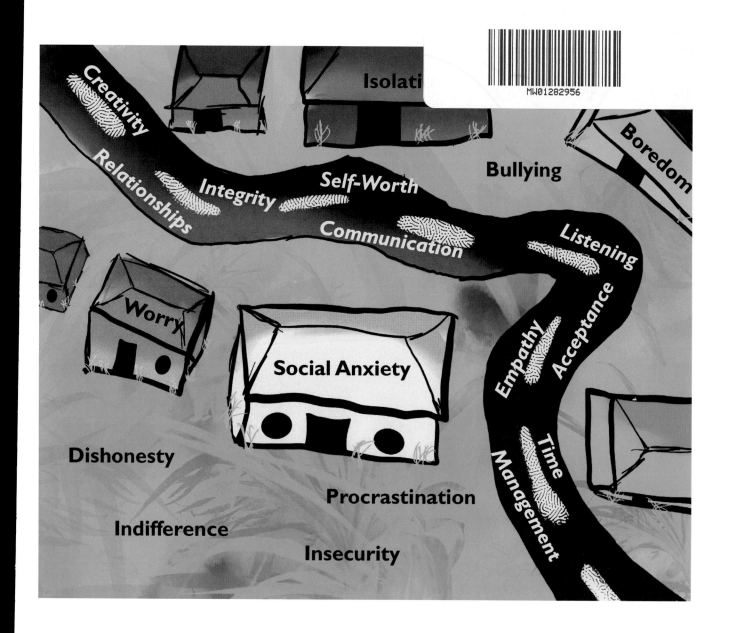

Creativity

Relationships

Integrity

Self-Worth

Isolati

Bullying

Boredom

Communication

Listening

Worry

Social Anxiety

Empathy

Acceptance

Dishonesty

Time Management

Procrastination

Indifference

Insecurity

A Road to Better Mental Health

A collection of original stories written and illustrated by teens for children...

Edited by Dr. Mary Jo Podgurski

Cover by Lily Gough (age 11)

©2022, MJ Podgurski, RNC, EdD, all rights reserved
ISBN 978-1-7343001-9-2
410 N. Main Street
Washington, Pa 15301
podmj@healthyteens.com

Dedication

This book is dedicated to the young authors and illustrators,
and to all young people.
#EachPersonIsAPersonofWorth

Acknowledgements

- Amy Podgurski Gough: The Adolescent Advisory Board was created in 1999; until 2021, I was it's coordinator. This year, I passed this program on to the capable, dedicated hands of my daughter, Amy Podgurski Gough. She leads this group and this effort beautifully and I am grateful.

- Landan Weakland: Landan is a peer educator alumnus and the supervisor of our Common Ground Teen Center; he supports Amy with the Advisory Board.

- Advisory Board Advisors: These good people are the foundation of the Board. Thank you.
  Suzanne Ashmore – Chartiers Houston High School
  Jessica Branagan – Washington High School
  Susan Humertson – Canon McMillan High School
  Alex Nikolopoulos – Avella High School
  Janet Toth – Charleroi High School
  Tiffani Trice-Kolar – Ringgold High School
  Nicole Welsh – Trinity High School

Thank You to Our Supporters

We are grateful to:

 **Staunton Farms Foundation,** for providing a start up grant of $5,000 for the project. The Foundation is dedicated to improving the lives of people who live with mental illness and/or substance use disorders.

The Foundation works to enhance behavioral health treatment and support by advancing best practices through grant making to non-profit organizations in ten southwestern Pennsylvania counties.

 **Washington Health System** is our collaborative partner and support since 1988. The goal at Washington Health System is to provide the community with an integrated healthcare system centered around patients and families that is comprised of leading medical experts, advanced technology and innovative procedures.

The Washington Health System's mission is Great Patient Care.

Washington County Behavioral Health and Developmental Services provides a portion of our Common Ground Teen Center's funding. The mission of the Washington County Behavioral Health and Developmental Services is to provide holistic, person-centered services and supports for infants, children, adolescents, and adults with Mental Health, Intellectual or Developmental Disabilities.

The number for the Washington County Crisis Line is 1-877-225-3567—it is available. 24 hours a day, 7 days a week, 365 days a year. The National Suicide Prevention Lifeline is 800-273-8255.

Why Talk about Mental Health?

I approach education wearing many hats—that of teacher, of course, but also from the perspective of nurse and counselor.

I am also 'seasoned', starting work as a pediatric RN at Children's Hospital in 1971. (I asked teens at a recent peer educator training to go into small groups where 'seasoned' educators matched with new trainees, and one of the teens asked me what type of seasoning was used!).

In over 50 years serving young people, I've witnessed adolescent angst, anxiety, and mental health issues, but the last years are unique. The U.S. Surgeon General issued a Advisory on Youth Mental Health Crisis on December 7, 2021 (see Appendix page 48).

Additionally, American Academy of Pediatrics, American Academy of Child and Adolescent Psychiatry and Children's Hospital Association issued a declaration of a national emergency in child and adolescent mental health in the fall of 2022 (page 48).

I wrote the 11th book in my Nonnie Series™ for children in 2021 to support trusted adults as they address these issues. I believe children and teens know more about the world around them than many adults think; I am certain open conversations about tough topics with adults in their lives eases discomfort and increases resilience.

Our teens wrote this book is one way older teens can reach out and educate children.

The Observer Reporter newspaper covered our book: https://observer-reporter.com/news/localnews/literary-lessons-teens-write-book-to-tackle-mental-health-challenges/article_27b94b1e-c016-11ec-a29d-8ba19101f085.html

Thank you for your support.

Mary Jo

Dr. Mary Jo Podgurski

Index of Stories

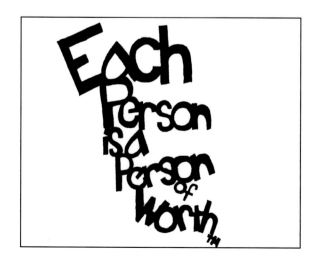

Liz's Big Worry!

Liz's Big Worry

Authors:

Laurel Bongioni

Shelby Loar

Illustrator:

Saundrah Chilzer

Avella School District Advisory Board Members

Story Topic:

Worry vs Listening

Story Objective:

At the end of the story, students will be able to:

- Share what it feels like to be worried about something.

Possible Discussion Questions:

1. What was Liz's big worry?

2. How did her friend Lane help her feel better?

Liz the lizard was always a worrisome little creature due to her size.

She was so tiny compared to her big home, the jungle.

One day, Liz told her best friend, Lane, about her fear of getting lost.

Lane took the time to listen to his friend's worries. Lane offered to help Liz by searching through the treetops to help Liz find her way home.

After talking to her friend, she thanked him for her help and felt better about her size in the forest.

Clocky Catches Up

Authors:

Nikki Zhang

Emma Hull

Illustrator:

Casey Ramirez

Canon McMillon
School District
Advisory Board Members

Story Topic:

Procrastination vs Time Management

Story Objective:

At the end of the story, students will be able to:

- Talk about at least one time when they put things off (procrastinated).

Possible Discussion Questions:

1. Why do you think Clocky was out of sync with the others?

2. What happened when he talked with his grandfather? Did it help him? Why or why not?

Clocky has a great life.

He gets up, goes to school, comes home, and goes to the park.

He spends maybe a little bit too much time at the park and this is starting to make him feel behind in school.

In this perfect school world, Clocky looks around and it seems like no one has the same problems as he does.

Everyone else's hands seem to be moving at a steady pace and this causes him to feel stressed because his hands are moving slower than the rest.

After school, feeling stressed, Clocky decides to go to the only place that makes him happy, the park. His parents and grandparents are starting to feel worried about him, so Clocky's grandpa goes to find him at the park.

After sitting on his swings and talking with his grandfather, Clocky seems to understand the importance of managing his time. His grandpa tells him that it is okay to go to the park, but that it is just as important to focus on school and family time at home.

Clocky and his grandfather decide that to get back on track, he can try a new routine. He will go to school and then instead of going straight to the park, he will come home and start on his school work. That way, he won't have to worry about school and fall behind. He can then go to the park and have fun.

Clocky put this plan to a start and started to see that his hands started to move at the right pace again, his grades were good again, and he still had time for the park!

Finn Finds His Truth

Authors:

Desiree Hancq

Ashley Horvath

Jack Lochran

Jake Mele

Cole Pawich

Elliott Wentzel

Illustrator:

Kelli Alderson

Chartiers Houston
School District
Advisory Board Members

 **Story Topic:**

Dishonesty vs Integrity

Story Objectives:

At the end of the story, students will be able to:

- Talk about what it means to be dishonest.

- Define integrity

Possible Discussion Questions:

1. Why do you think Finn lied?

2. This is a magical town. What do you think the bee represents?

It was Mother's Day in Finn's magical town! He went to the flower shop in town to pick up a special flower for his Mom.

Finn picked out a beautiful flower for his mother. It had 6 petals, each a different color! Finn began walking home through the magical town. On his way home, a man asked Finn where he got such a beautiful flower. Finn spoke back to the man and said, "I grew it myself!"

When Finn said this, the red petal on his flower turned gray and fell to the ground. Everything red in Finn's world turned gray, too. Finn was sad about this but kept walking home. Another man asked Finn where he got his flower. Again, Finn said, "I grew it myself!"

Suddenly, the blue petal on Finn's flower turned gray and fell to the ground. All the blue in Finn's world faded to gray. Finn was very upset and did not know what was happening. A woman came up to Finn and asked him where he got his flower. Finn, for the third time, said, "I grew it myself!"

As Finn told this lie for the third time, the last four petals turned gray and fell off of his flower. Everything in Finn's world faded to gray, and he was left with only the flower's stem.

Finn started to cry. A bee flew up to Finn to collect pollen. Finn's flower was dead, though. When the bee saw the dead flower, he knew Finn had been lying. The wise bee explained to Finn that he needed to tell the truth. Finn understood. The bee asked Finn where he got his beautiful flower. Finally, Finn replied, "I got it from the flower shop in town."

When Finn told the truth, all 6 of the colored petals on his flower sprouted back up. Finn was able to see all the color in his world again! He thanked the bee for teaching him to tell the truth. Finn ran home to give his mother the flower.

At last, Finn made it home to surprise his mother with the beautiful flower for Mother's Day. Finn's Mom joyfully raised her arms up to give Finn a big hug.

Oliver Takes a Chance

Authors:

Mackenzie Figolah
Grace Hutchin

Leah Stein

Illustrator:

Leah Stein

Charleroi School District
Advisory Board Members

 ## Story Topic:

Isolation vs Relationships

Story Objective:

At the end of the story, students will be able to:

- Share an experience when it was difficult to make friends.

Possible Discussion Questions:

1. Oliver was afraid but also lonely. Why do you think he was afraid?

2. Was Annie a good friend?

3. How do you think Oliver felt when Annie pushed him?

There once was a lonely owl named Oliver. Each night he looked down from his tall tree at the other animals in the busy forest, but he was too shy to fly down and make friends with them.

He had one friend, another owl named Annie. She didn't like that Oliver was lonely. She often tried to get him to meet the other creatures but he was always too scared and said, "Maybe."

Oliver became even shyer as time went on and wouldn't even visit Annie.

Annie became very worried about Oliver's loneliness and went over that night. She tried to show him that he needed to make friends. Oliver still felt too nervous.

But as Oliver was saying "Maybe," she pushed him out of his tree and flew after him. Oliver was so surprised that he flew straight down into the forest.

He was very frightened as the other animals came over to meet him but Annie introduced each one.

Oliver found that he had a lot in common with the other animals. He liked to fly over the lake just like Harold the hawk. He liked to play in the trees just like Rilla the squirrel. And Art the hedgehog was nervous about meeting new people, just like Oliver!

Annie was proud of Oliver for being brave and meeting her friends. And Oliver was proud of himself for coming down from his tree. He had learned that it was much better to meet new friends, even if it was scary, than to stay in his tree and be lonely. He couldn't wait to see his new friends again!

Darcy Fits In

Authors:

Elizabeth Brison

Rowan Curry

Dylen Knox

Brycen McAdoo

Illustrator:

Brycen McAdoo

Teen Outreach
Peer Educators

 ## Story Topic:
Bullying vs Empathy

Story Objectives:

At the end of the story, students will be able to:

- Define bullying.

- Define empathy.

Possible Discussion Questions:

1. Do you think most new students feel nervous before they go to school for the first time?

2. Why did Darcy feel better when the teacher arrived?

Once upon a time, there was a poison dart frog named Darcy.

Darcy was starting a new school and was very nervous.

They were worried that they would be the only frog that wasn't smooth and green.

When Darcy got off the bus, and walked into class, all the frogs turned and stared at them.

Some frogs started laughing at them.
One frog came up to them and called them mean names.

Darcy felt very defeated and wished they hadn't come to school at all.

That was, until the teacher hopped into the room.

The bully stopped in his tracks as the moss frog took his seat at the teacher's desk.

The two unique frogs looked at each other and Darcy felt accepted in the classroom.

Create Your Own Story Step 1:

Would you like to write your own story?

The first step is to decide the topic of your story.

A writer first needs to imagine the story. This could happen while you're on your way to and from school, or when you're falling asleep, or when you're sitting outside on a nice day.

Then, it helps to create a storyboard.

Creating a storyboard often helps.

A storyboard might look like this:

Character	Concept	Illustration

Daisy's Adventure

Authors:

Gianni Cantini

Jack Duncan

Kirra Gerard

Kelley Kulp

Donte Newton

Krenna Rahr

Kensi Staffen

Martina Stasko

Illustrator:

Aleah Siwula

Ringgold School District
Board Members

 ## Story Topic:

Boredom vs Creativity

Story Objective:

At the end of the story, students will be able to:

- List at least two ways to move away from feeling bored.

Possible Discussion Questions:

1. Have you ever felt bored?

2. What did Daisy do to feel creative?

3. Do you think being creative helps with boredom?

Daisy is bored.

She is tired and doesn't know what to do.

Daisy gets an idea!

"Why don't I paint something and try something new?"

Daisy learned how fun it was to be creative, so she wants to share it with her friends outside.

Daisy found what she was good at, tried something new, and she shared her ideas with friends and family.

 **Create Your Own Story, Step 2**

Write the story!

This is your story—write what inspires you and makes you happy. Your voice is important!

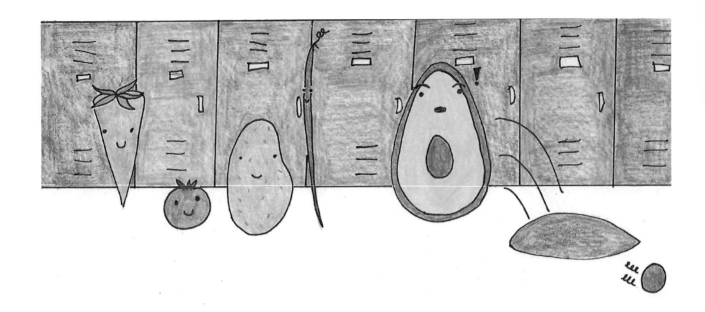

Ariana Avocado's First Day at School

Authors:

Isaiah Dale

Brookelyn Dames

Merielle DiGregory

Adelle Hollowood

Hunter Jenkins

Bailey Wheeler

Illustrators:

Rowan Curry

Merielle DiGregory

Adelle Hollowood

Common Ground Teen Center Members

Story Topic:

Social Anxiety vs Communication

Story Objectives:

At the end of the story, students will be able to:

- Define social anxiety

- Name at least two ways talking about anxiety can help.

Possible Discussion Questions:

1. Why was Ariana stressed after she fell?

2. How did Ariana's friends help her?

3. What does it mean if someone 'has your back'?

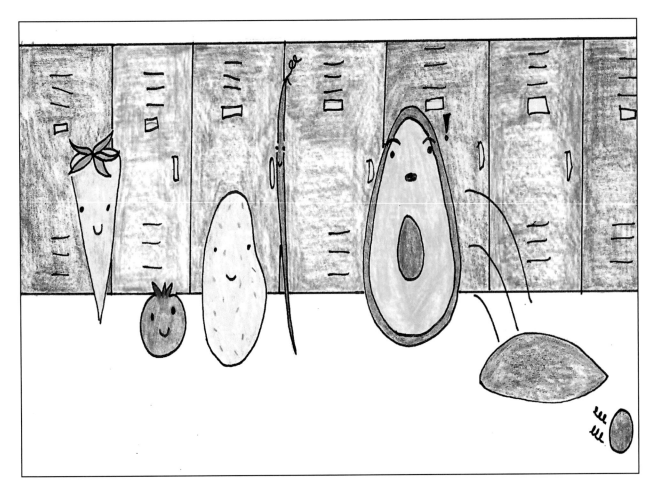

It is Ariana's first day at a new school after moving from a different town.

She was walking down the hall with her friend, Alex, on their way to the cafeteria for lunch, when she fell flat on her face!

A couple of strangers see that she has fallen; Meredith, Monica, and Jim go over to help her. She gets flustered as they try to help her and her stress builds up.

Alex follows her out and tries to comfort her. As she starts to calm down, Meredith, Monica and Jim arrive to make sure that she is okay.

Ariana assures them she is fine, just embarrassed by the situation and explains she gets really nervous around new people.

Ariana describes her social anxiety like sinking in quicksand. The group encourages Ariana and tell her they have her back.

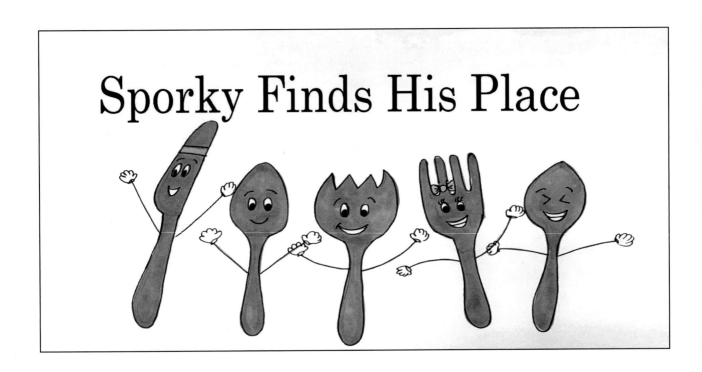

Sporky Finds His Place

Authors:

Emma Bowman,

Hannah Eisiminger

Olivia Herrnberger

Miranda Rinehart

Emily Tuite

Illustrator:

Selah Taggart

Trinity School District
Board Members

 **Story Topic:**

Indifference vs Acceptance

Story Objectives:

At the end of the story, students will be able to:

- Discuss the idea of acceptance.

- Explain what it means to feel left out.

Possible Discussion Questions:

1. What did you think about Sporky's first time in the cafeteria?

2. How did Sporky's parents help?

3. If you were Sporky, how would you feel?

All was calming down in the house of the Maes. Sporky was preparing for his first day of middle school. Sporky had his first day jitters, he was not sure he was going to fit in, but as mom and dad tucked him in, his worries seemed to go away.

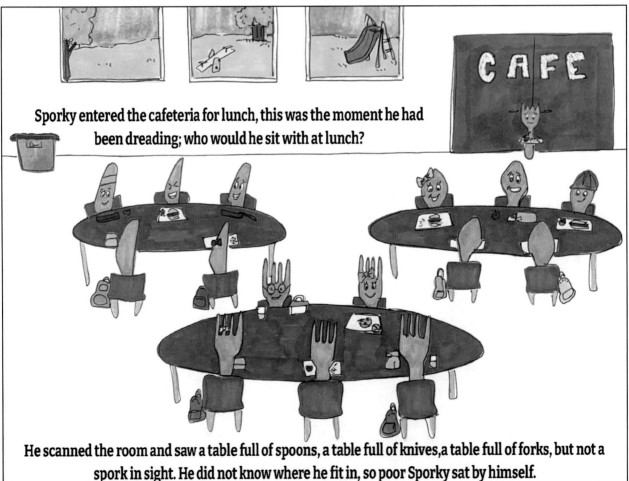

Sporky entered the cafeteria for lunch, this was the moment he had been dreading; who would he sit with at lunch?

He scanned the room and saw a table full of spoons, a table full of knives, a table full of forks, but not a spork in sight. He did not know where he fit in, so poor Sporky sat by himself.

That evening, the Macs sat down for their family dinner. Sporky was unusually quiet. Dad began to question Sporky on his day. Sporky's eyes began to tear up as he explained his day; for he felt like he didn't fit in with the other kids. Mom explains that everyone is different and you need to find similarities to make a connection. Dad said it's okay to be a little different because no one is exactly the same.

The next day at school, Sporky walked in with a new attitude. Sporky walked over to the table of forks and introduced himself. He complimented the forks on their long prongs and pointed out his little prongs. The forks invited him to sit down and began to ask questions about his unique roundness. Sporky finally felt he belonged.

Jayden Makes His Shot

Authors:

Eden Day

Amara Garrett

Mareesa Garrett

Diana Jandres

Issiah Patterson

Illustrator:

Willow Maffio

Washington School District
Board Members

 ## Story Topic:

Insecurity vs Worthiness

Story Objectives:

At the end of the story, students will be able to:

- Define what it means to feel insecure

- Discuss self-worth

Possible Discussion Questions:

1. Jayden's confidence is low as he attempts his shot. Why do you think he feels insecure?

2. Is Jayden worthy whether or not he makes his shot?

Jayden is new to the basketball team this year. This is the first game where Jayden gets the chance to play along with his teammates.

He gets the ball, and he is ready to shoot, only to miss his shot.

Immediately, he feels embarrassed and disappointed because his teammate Mark is making fun of him for missing his shot.

Half-time approaches and the couch approaches him before he goes into the locker room. The coach reassures him that he is a new player and can not make every shot. The second half of the game is on, and Jayden gets back on the game. He gets the ball to shoot only this time he makes it. Jayden instantly feels a boost of self-confidence and happiness.

Create Your Own Story Step 3:

Illustrate your story!

Art is very personal.

Let your pictures tell your story.

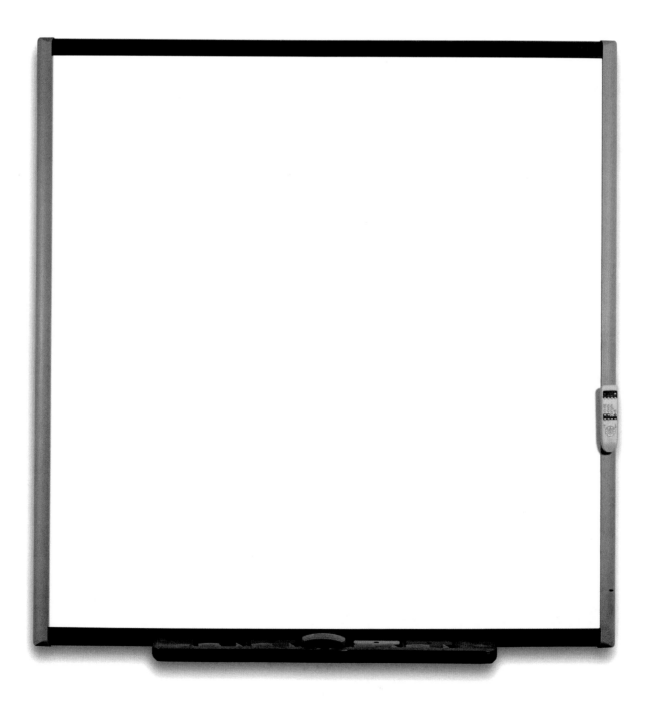

Appendix 1:

About the Washington Health System Teen Outreach Youth Programs

Founded in 1988, the Washington Health System Teen Outreach hosts seven youth programs. Three programs are involved in the A Road to Mental Health Book Project:

1. The Adolescent Advisory Board:

Created in 1999, the Board consists of teens from local school districts.

 An annual youth conference is held each spring, during which the Board members teach other teens topics they develop using learning stations. We call this Speed Learning!

2. Peer Education:

This program trains teens to teach younger teens and was started in 1995. Over 15,000 teens have been trained as peer educators.

3. The Common Ground Teen Center:

The Center was opened in 2008.
It is teen driven and run by teen employees.

The Center offers ten clubs, like Cooking Club, Banned Book Club, and Art Club. It is open M - F, 4 - 8 PM.

For information on these programs, email Dr. Mary Jo at podmj@healthyteens.com

Appendix 2:
Resources:

A Declaration from the American Academy of Pediatrics, American Academy of Child and Adolescent Psychiatry and Children's Hospital Association:

https://www.aap.org/en/advocacy/child-and-adolescent-healthy-mental-development/aap-aacap-cha-declaration-of-a-national-emergency-in-child-and-adolescent-mental-health/

U.S. Surgeon General Issues Advisory on Youth Mental Health Crisis Further Exposed by COVID-19 Pandemic:

https://www.hhs.gov/about/news/2021/12/07/us-surgeon-general-issues-advisory-on-youth-mental-health-crisis-further-exposed-by-covid-19-pandemic.html

Text of full Surgeon General's Advisory on Protecting Youth Mental Health:

https://www.hhs.gov/sites/default/files/surgeon-general-youth-mental-health-advisory.pdf

Nonnie Talks about Mental Health:
http://bit.ly/NonnieMentalHealth

Made in the USA
Middletown, DE
30 April 2022

65044602R00031